Before God spoke anything into existence
THE DEEP EXISTED

INTO THE
DEEP

RHODA OBIRI YEBOAH

I0358750

LIFE AND SUCCESS PUBLISHING
www.abookinsideyou.com

Copyright © 2019 Rhoda Obiri Yeboah

All rights reserved. No part of this publication may be produced, distributed, or transmitted in any form or by any means, including photocopying, recording, or other electronic or mechanical methods, without the prior written permision of the publisher, except in the case of brief quotations embodied in critical reviews and certain other noncommercial uses permitted by copyright law.

For permission requests, write to the publisher, addressed "Attention: Permissions Coordinator" at the email address below:

Life and Success Media Ltd

e-mail: info@abookinsideyou.com

www.abookinsideyou.com

Unless otherwise stated, all scripture quotations are taken from the Holy Bible, New King James Version. Quotations marked NKJV are taken from the HOLY BIBLE, NEW KING JAMES VERSION. Copyright © 1973, 1978, 1984 by International Bible Society. Used by permission of Hodder and Stoughton Ltd, a member of the Hodder Headline Plc Group. All rights reserved. "NKJV" is a registered trademark of International Bible Society. UK trademark number 1448790.

Quotations marked KJV are from the Holy Bible,

King James Version.

Cover Design: **mia**design.com

ISBN: 978-1-64764-756-8

Contents

Foreword 5

Acknowledgement 7

Preface 9

Introduction 11

1. Deep Call For Deep 15

2. Disobedience 25

3. God Reveals 35

Into The Deep

Foreword

Rhoda Obiri Yeboah's love for God is clearly seen in her book, "INTO THE DEEP." This is an encouragement into intimacy with God. For you to enjoy the hidden riches of God. Rhoda invites the reader to come into the deep places of God and enjoy the deep riches of Him.

She uses scripture to show us clearly that God is deep and to enjoy His unsearchable riches; we need to get into the deep places with Him. Rhoda has searched the scriptures in several translations to give us a rich tapestry of the God we serve and His desire for deep fellowship with His children.

The last chapter is an amazing revelation of God's love for us and His deep yearning for our love. Captivating read! I am privileged to be Rhoda's pastor and can testify to the fact that she lives what she preaches. I pray that you will get into the spirit of this book to transform your fellowship with the Living God. Enjoy Into The Deep.

– Rev. Martin Ossei,
Senior Pastor, **Joyhouse London**

Acknowledgement

To God be the glory. I bless my Father, God, for His grace and His Spirit that rests on me and are at work in my life. I thank Him for pouring into me to share His riches stored for those who fear and seek Him.

I bless God for my family. My husband, Edwin for being a unique individual. My children, Russell, Winston, Maya, you inspire me by reading and encouraging me. My dad, Rev Yaw Obiri Yeboah, you taught me well, thank you. My mum, grandma, sisters, brother, you are all a true blessing. Thank you and God bless you.

To my Senior Pastor, Martin Ossei, for the depth of God you teach, taking the time to read and correct this script. Thank you, and God bless you.

All Joy house Pastors and leaders, you are amazing. Prophet D. K. Isaac, thank you for everything.

Preface

In Genesis 1:1-2, we understand that darkness covers the surface of the deep. And in verse 3, God spoke (sound to words) light into existence. God never created light. He commanded it to manifest. That is the power of the words we speak; it can create. Can I disclose to you that light was in the darkness? Light was present with darkness until God commanded light to separate itself from darkness and shine. Light shines! The (sound) words from a child of God can be distinctive because of the power at work in us (Romans 8:11). Until you know and believe you are light, meant to shine, you will allow darkness to dwell with you.

In all of us dwell an amount of darkness (because of sin) and light. But we are called to separate ourselves and dominate. You are a well of depths — deep truths of God's goodness. Nations are entrusted to you. Deep revelations. The strength to overtake and conquer lies in the depth of you. If you allow the truth of God's word to separate the light from the darkness in you, it will reach the deep that is covered in the inside of you.

In this era, God is calling us to seek Him as a person. The person of love and truth. The Holy Ghost will help and guide us in our walk as children of light. The Holy Spirit will take what the Father's will for us is and make it known to us (John 16:13). Jesus paid the price for our redemption. He took our place that we will be made whole through our belief in His birth and resurrection so we can walk and dominate in victory.

Nothing stops you from becoming great in your field of calling and election. Nothing can stand in your way when you know what lies dormant inside of you waiting to come forth. Launch up into the deep, bring out the purpose for which your life is apprehended.

Introduction

God has many sons (the human race). Any individual who has accepted and confessed the Lord Jesus as his saviour is adopted into the household of God and has become co-heir with Christ (Romans 8:17). It is called Salvation, and it is a gift from God (Ephesians 2:8). You receive this gift by believing in the finished work of the cross by Jesus, who is the Christ.

> *"But to all who believed him and accepted him, he gave the right to become children of God. They are reborn – not with a physical birth resulting from human passion or plan, but a birth that comes from God"*
> *(John 1:12-13 NLT).*

I live in the United Kingdom. When a child is born to a British parent, the child automatically becomes a British citizen, and that is by birth. You earn all the rights of the British because of being born by British parents. So, it is in the kingdom of God, when you believe in the existence of God and accepts Jesus His Son as the only truth and life. And confess with your mouth that He died in your stead – He gives you the right to become a citizen of heaven! And that is a Gift. You don't earn it; you don't work for it; you only believe to become one.

This is the simplicity of the ways of God, our Father (1 John 3:1), His Word, which is forever potent and true that is Jesus (John 1:1 and 14), and the Holy Spirit who is ever-present, our help and Advocate (John 14:26). He is the power working in the children of obedience. This promise is our truth. This makes a child of God a force to be reckoned with. Yet the truth of who we are in Christ is not easy for most to grasp, even children of the light.

"Then Jesus exclaimed, "Father, thank you, for you are Lord, the supreme Ruler over heaven and earth! And you have hidden the great revelation of your authority from those who are proud and wise in their own eyes. Instead, you have shared it with those who humble themselves" (Mathew 11:25 TPT).

Introduction

It always brings me to the place of humility and reverence of the King of kings when I read verses like this in the Bible. God, our Father, does not give "His Authority" to just anyone. Neither does He reveal His great revelation to the proud. He knows revelation knowledge is powerful, so He is discreet in whom He would entrust such truths that can change nations.

We are spirit beings, and our spirits thrive on revelation. Revelation is the meat of the spirit! We as human beings, are made of spirit, soul, and body. Christians believe we are spirit and that is what should rule or be dominant in our lives. That is living by the spirit. The Holy Spirit is a spirit; we communicate with him in spirit and manifest Him in the flesh or body. You do not take what is flesh and make it spiritual it will be out of order!

> *"But the things that come out of the mouth comes from the heart, and these things defile a man"*
> *(Matthew 15:18).*

It is not always what you have processed in your heart that defines or defiles you. It is what comes out of you and not what you put in, although that also has its effect.

> *"A man is not defiled by what enters his mouth, but by what comes out of it." (Mathew 15:11)*

Therefore, it is prudent to be conscious of what you allow to enter you. You only become what you feed on. Grow your spirit with the things of God, and you won't gratify the desires of your flesh (Galatians 5:16). Watch out what comes out of you; your sound determines what you are made of. Your sound informs who rules over your life. And your words show what you feed on.

Chapter 1

Deep Calls For Deep

Psalm 42:7 Aramaic Bible in Plain English "The Deep to deep calls The Voice to the voice of the waters of your fountains. All your storms and your waves passed over me." Before I touch on the verse above, let me take you to Genesis 1:2 King James Bible,

"And the earth was without form, and void, and darkness was upon the face of the deep. And the Spirit of God moved upon the face of the waters."

I want to enlighten your spirit to something.

Before God started to speak anything into existence, The Deep existed!

Christian Standard Bible *"Now, the earth was formless and empty, darkness covered the surface of the watery depths, and the Spirit of God was hovering over the surface of the waters."*

Contemporary English Version *"The earth was barren, with no form of life; it was under a roaring ocean covered with darkness. But the Spirit of God was moving over the water."*

International Standard Version *"When the earth was as yet unformed and desolate, with the surface of the ocean depths shrouded in darkness, and while the Spirit of God was hovering over the surface of the waters."*

All these versions depict that there was a depth that was covered by darkness. And may I divulge to you that these depths are the depths of the spirit that is available to us if we will press in with the truth of God available to us. That is the Word of God. The CSB said watery depth, water is a symbolic representation of the work of the Holy Spirit in the word of God. But realise that the Spirit Hovers over this deep. In the beginning, I brought about the secret of the Lord belongs to those who fear Him and diligently seek Him. To those who humble themselves under Him. Unless you are in the posture of humility, and with the fear of God, there are depths of Him you will never Know!

"He set the earth on its foundations, never to be moved. You covered it with the deep like a garment; the waters stood above the mountains" (Psalm 104:5-6).

The Lord does cover His deep things, but it is there to be discovered if we seek it with all our hearts.

"You will seek me and find me when you seek me with all your heart" (Jeremiah 29:13).

I will be found by you, declares the LORD, and I will restore you from captivity and gather you from all nations and places to which I have banished you, declares the LORD. I will restore you to the place from which I sent you into exile." (Jeremiah 29:14).

The Lord desires that we seek Him because he made us for fellowship with Himself. To restore to us what the enemy stole from us through Eve's disobedience.

"I thought to myself, 'I would love to treat you as my own children!' I wanted nothing more than to give you this beautiful land – the finest possession in the world. I looked forward to your calling me 'Father,' and I wanted you to never turn from me" (Jeremiah 3:19 NLT)

The Lord Almighty, the possessor of heaven and earth so desired to treat us like His children (this is before Christ Jesus came to die on the cross) – to give us the very best of the earth, our possessions.

He will do anything to hear you call Him Father. Selah.

No wonder when the disciples ask Jesus to teach them how to pray (Mathew 6:9-13). He said when you pray, say, Our Father …. Remember, throughout the scriptures, that was the only time the disciples ask Jesus to teach them something. Prayer is a communication with our father. Do you hear Him when you pray? Selah

He never wants to let you go! If we are going to discern the mind of God, we need intimacy, humility, and the Word of God. Also, His spirit to take what is his and made it known to us.

The LORD, our God, has secrets known to no one. We are not accountable for them, but our children and we are accountable forever for all that he has revealed to us, so that we may obey all the terms of these instructions.

Into The Deep

"Now that this truth is revealed to you, you are accountable if you do not hold on and run with it" Selah! (Deuteronomy 29:29 NLT)

The Voice to the voice that call is when you are intimate with the Lord, you are one with Him as the mystery of a man and his wife when they become one (when the man carnally knows his wife). It is so with the Lord; His word is in you so richly that what comes out of you is His word. His voice is your voice.

"The Deep to deep calls The Voice to the voice of the waters of your fountains. All your storms and your waves passed over me" (Psalm 42:7).

The depth of our Lord is calling for the depth of us; His Spirit is calling for our spirit to meet at the fountain. When we meet with Him intimately in our secret place, He promises to reveal unto us a depth of Himself no one knows. A part of Him that you need at that particular season of your life, this is where the word of God becomes real to you when it says you will yield fruit in season and will never wither, and whatever you doeth will prosper (Psalm 1:3).

I will send you the seasonal rains. The land will then yield its crops, and the trees of the field will produce their fruit (Leviticus 26:4).

That is His promise.

You sent abundant rain, O God; You refreshed Your weary inheritance (Psalm 68:9).

The LORD will indeed provide what is good, and our land will yield its increase (Psalm 85:12).

The LORD shall open unto thee his good treasure, the heaven to give the rain unto thy land in his season, and to bless all the work of thine hand: and thou shalt lend unto many nations, and thou shalt not borrow. Amen (Deuteronomy 28:12).

But, remember all his storms and waves will pass over you. Praise God. What does that mean? We are also baptized into His suffering.

"But I have a baptism of suffering to go through. And I must go through it" (Luke 12:50).

It is a must that you and I MUST go through these storms and waves!

Romans 6:3 says, *"All of us were baptized into Christ Jesus. Don't you know that we were baptized into his death? We have the same baptism of Christ. For as many of you as were baptized into Christ have put on Christ."*

To the Children of God writes, "Behold what manner of love the Father has given to us, that we should be called children of God. And that is what we are! The reason the world does not know us is that it did not know Him. Beloved, we are now children of God, and what we will be has not yet been revealed. We know that when Christ appears, we will be like Him, for we will see Him as He is. And everyone who has this hope in Him purifies himself, just as Christ is pure… (Galatians 3:7).

1 John 3:1-3 Berean Study Bible You are a child of God! The Father Loves you! That is why the world does not know you! Because it did not know Him!

WHAT YOU WILL BE HAS NOT YET BEEN REVEALED!!!

Anyone with this hope Purifies Himself just as Christ is! Hallelujah Amen

Don't wait till Christ appears in glory to look like Him. When you believe and accept Jesus, confess he is Lord over your life, accept His life, and His nature. The old nature is no more. Now you are Christ (Christian) and a child of God. Just as Jesus is, so are you. Whatever Jesus can do, you can do too. As you dwell in the sanctuary and behold Him, you shall grow from glory to glory. The Glory of the New Covenant

> *"Have this attitude in yourselves which was also in Christ Jesus" (Philippians 2:5 NASB).*

> *"They do not know or understand; they wander in the darkness; all the foundations of the earth are shaken."*
> *I have said, "You are gods; you are all sons of the Most High (Psalm 82:5-6).*

Because we do not understand who we are, that we are gods, we wander in darkness (identity crisis). Not knowing what we carry and whose we are. No wonder the whole earth is groaning and waiting for the manifestation of the sons of God (Romans 8:19). You are a child of God, walk and live as Royalty! Amen

> *Now the Lord is the Spirit, and where the Spirit of the Lord is, there is freedom. 18And we, who with unveiled faces all reflect the glory of the Lord, are being transformed into His image with intensifying glory, which comes from the Lord, who is the Spirit.*
> *(2 Corinthians 3:17 Berean Study Bible)*
> *Selah.*

Chapter 2

Disobedience

The first sin, which is DISOBEDIENCE, as subtle as it is, works in all of us. How? Anytime we choose to ignore the Word of God, we will forget to do what it says. It contributes to our ignoring the prompting of the Holy Spirit. The channel for the introduction of sin in any form is a process.

"No temptation has overtaken you except what is common to mankind" (1 Corinthians 10: 13a NIV).

The way of familiarity makes us careless because we, as human beings, feel it is ok. In the garden of Eden, Eve had a conversation with the snake. I believe at the inception of creation Adam and Eve had a pleasant relationship with all creation, whereby there was a way of communication. Because of this familiarity, Eve did not see the harm in having a conversation with the snake.

"Now the serpent was more subtle than any beast of the field which the Lord God had made" (Genesis 3:1a BRG).

Most of the different translations of the Bible use the word shrewd to describe how the serpent is in nature. The serpent is shred; (subtle), meaning it is crafty or prudent, cunning, and cautious, to mention a few. These, bear in mind are the same description of the devil our enemy. The bible has already told us in 1 Corinthians 10:13 that every way or process of what tempts us is common to us. This is to set as a guide for us to know and be sensitive to walk in the right path of life. It is also necessary to point out why the Holy Spirit prompts us of things to come because He knows of things to come. He is the Spirit of truth, All-Knowing God. He is our guide in this life. We all have two sides of influences in our life, whether you like it or not: The influence of the subtle serpent and that of the Holy Spirit. These influences have an environment that they grow in.

> *"What delight comes to those who follow God's ways! They won't walk in step with the wicked, nor share the sinner's way, nor be found sitting in the scorner's seat. Their pleasure and passion are remaining true to the Word of "I Am," meditating day and night in his true revelation of light" (Psalm 1:1 TPT)*

KJV version *"Blessed is the man that walketh not in the counsel of the ungodly, nor standeth in the way of sinners, nor sitteth in the seat of the scornful. But his delight is in the law of the Lord; and in his law doth he meditates day and night."*

The bible makes it plain the blessed state of the one who follows God's ways. The one who follows the Spirits leading will not follow the steps of the wicked nor share in the sinner's ways. Neither will he be found sitting in the seat of the scornful (the feeling or expressing contempt) (Psalm 1:2). We are called to love; love is the language of the Spirit of life. Your passion is to be true to the word of God – Meditating on it day and night, which brings your spirit, God's deposit in you, revelation light to his word (Rhema). Translating to wisdom for your daily walk. You will find your victory in the word.

> *"They will be standing firm like a flourishing tree planted by God's design, deeply rooted by the brooks of bliss, bearing fruit in every season of their lives. They are never dry, never fainting, ever blessed, ever prosperous"*
>
> *(Psalm 1:3)*

God promises you this abundant life in return. A blessed state of life. Bearing fruit in every season of life, never lacking. That is God's way of living. But this is only possible when you are deeply rooted in God by the brooks of bliss "the joy of the Lord, that is your strength" (Nehemiah 8:10). Being joyous in life makes you fruitful through every season of life. You will bear fruit because you are rooted and planted by the river of life.

Disobedience

"Who has believed our message, to whom has the Lord revealed his powerful arm? (Isaiah 53:1 NLT)

This is the message that we believe; the covenant of God we proclaim. This is God's ideal for mankind, but we missed this providential way when the serpent deceived Eve in Eden. So, my brethren, I beg you by the mercies of God, be obedient to what God is opening up to us, harness your emotions to the things of God, live for Him, let Him have the reigns of your life. Do not let the serpent of our days, which manifests through the distractions around us deceive you into disobeying what the Spirit says to the children of God. Now the Bible gives us this report;

"All of us, like sheep, have strayed away. We have left God's paths to follow our own. Yet the Lord laid on him the sins of us all" (Isaiah 53:6).

Isaiah, the prophet expresses that we all have strayed from the will of God for our lives because we are conceived and born in sin (Psalm 51:5). We left

God's path to follow our selfish desires. But the flesh has nothing good in it. You cannot trust your flesh to make good decisions. The path God desired for us has already been predestined. It can only come to us if we follow His leading and abide in Him.

"For I know that in me (that is, in my flesh) nothing good dwells; for to will is present with me, but how to perform what is good I do not find" (Romans 7:18 NKJV).

It clearly says I have a will to do what is right, yet I cannot perform it because my flesh by nature can't do good! In Luke 18:19, Jesus expressed, no one is good except God. In our flesh, good cannot be extracted; good comes from God. We have a deposit of him that is His Spirit. He has given as a witness to bear testimony with our spirit of things to come. God is the only good! We can only be victorious if we live by the spirit and not gratify the desires of the flesh.

"However, when He, the Spirit of truth, has come, He will guide you into all truth; for He will not speak on His own

authority, but whatever He hears He will speak; and He will tell you things to come. He will glorify Me, for He will take of what is Mine and declare it to you. All things that the Father has are Mine. Therefore, I said that He will take of Mine and declare it to you"

(John 16:13-15 NKJV).

The Spirit of God is the truth bearer. He is the only one that guides us into all truth! He never speaks of Himself but everything that the Father speaks. He aims to glorify God through the finished work of Jesus Christ. He declares what is ours through Christ to us. He directs the way to providence. Our path is to have faith and obey. 2 Corinthians 10: 6 says, "When our obedience is complete, he will punish every disobedience." Our part in this is to believe God, have faith in his Word, do what it says, and He will glorify Himself.

"The Spirit himself testifies with our spirit that we are God's children. Now if we are children, then we are heirs—heirs of God and co-heirs with Christ, if indeed we share in his sufferings in order that we may also share in his glory. I consider that our present sufferings are

not worth comparing with the glory that will be revealed in us. For the creation waits in eager expectation for the children of God to be revealed" (Romans 8:16-19 NIV).

Verse 16 emphasises our true stature as a child of God. We are His heir as Jesus is. If we share in the suffering of Christ, we have a part in his glory too. This world is full of troubles, but we are overcomers because Christ overcame and said, "it is finished" on the cross.

1 John 4:4 Contemporary English Version writes; *"Children, you belong to God, and you have defeated these enemies. God's Spirit is in you and is more powerful than the one who is in the world."*

We belong to God and have His spirit that walks us in victory. Remember, we stand in victory. As children of God, let us stand in that position of strength and win this battle to the glory of God.

Verse 18 tells us nothing that we suffer in the name of Christ is compared to what shall be revealed in us. Anything we go through as a child of God is designed to bring out or reveal God in us and to us. Creation waits for us to be manifested, not only when Jesus appears again in glory to rapture us, but anytime we take a stand for what we believe and are willing to be crucified and suffer for the truth we believe in, we are manifested as children of light. The secret to the strength of God is obedience.

The devil is only afraid of your submission to the council of heaven. Know the word of God; that is the truth. The truth is what moves heaven. The word of God is Jesus personified John 1:14, *"He is the only way, the truth and the life."* Let us obey this truth and do us it says, and our victory is assured.

Into The Deep

Chapter 3

God Reveals

God in His sovereignty chooses whom to reveal Himself to, and it is to the humble and those who fear him (reverential fear).

> *"The secret of the LORD is with those who fear Him,*
> *And He will show them His covenant"*
> *(Psalm 25:14 NKJV).*

It is the choice of God to reveal to whom He so desires, but for you to be in that position, you need humility. Humility is the gateway to the revelations of God. God hates the proud!

"But he gives us even more grace to stand against such evil desires. As the Scriptures say, "God opposes the proud but favors the humble"

(James 4:6).

As the Scriptures say, "God opposes the proud but favors the humble." God's favour is with the humble. He gives more grace to know and do for His pleasure. Look at this verse carefully; Good News Translation of the same verse; "But the grace that God gives is even stronger. As the scripture says, "God resists the proud, but gives grace to the humble." The grace for the humble is even stronger to do exploits. God resists the proud.

Sometimes when we sense we are being resisted in life, we need to sit back and reflect on our life if there is any pride in us and repent of it. For all you know, it is God Himself resisting you. Selah!

What is humility then? The dictionary defines humility as ``the quality of having a modest or low view of one's importance." But I love how C. S. Lewis defines it; 'Humility is not thinking less of yourself; it is thinking of yourself less.' And that is exactly how God wants us to think, thinking more of Him and less of ourselves after all our lives have already been predestined that we should walk in.

"Therefore let us have the mind of Christ so we can please God, don't think of yourself higher than you ought to"
(Ephesians 2:10).

Again, I love how The Passion Translation says it; "There's a private place reserved for the lovers of God, where they sit near him and receive the revelation-secrets of his promises" (Psalm 25:14). Hallelujah! Praise God. If you desire to know the secrets of God, become His lover! Have a secret place where you meet, and He would share his secrets with you. God desired to be pursued like a lover. It always delights my heart that He is the lover of my soul. He is the one who has the seat of my affection before my husband and children. God is the lover of my life!

"You are my private garden, my treasure, my bride, a secluded spring, a hidden fountain" Selah
(Songs of Solomon 4:12 NLT).

This is how the Almighty God sees you and has made you, His private garden. You know how people spend quality time with their gardens, uprooting every weed one by one. They know every detail of the garden. They are aware of what they desire to see in the garden, what to grow, when to grow, what to uproot, and what nutrients to provide. Hallelujah. That is what God desires to have with you. His garden. Your life.

Treasure is defined as several precious metals, gems, or other valuable objects: not just any precious metal but quantity. You are a heavyweight gem; no wonder hell pursues you and your desires. You are His. He calls you My treasure. When you have an expensive necklace, as a woman, I will relate to that; you don't wear it just anyhow. You wear it on special occasions. You wear it with pride! Because you know it's worth. That is exactly how God feels and want to boast in you. His treasure.

> *"Then the LORD asked Satan, "Have you noticed my servant Job? He is the finest man in all the earth. He is blameless--a man of complete integrity. He fears God and stays away from evil" (Job 1:8 NLT)*

This verse always gives me chills when I read. "Have you noticed my servant Job?" Elohim asked Satan. It's like you asking your friends, haven't you noticed my quality, precious, beautiful, elegant necklace? Everyone wants a compliment when they have something of worth to display, so is God. You are His inheritance,

> *"For the LORD'S portion is his people;*
> *Jacob is the lot of his inheritance"*
> *(Deuteronomy 32:9).*

May He find you worthy of His boast to Satan. You are His treasure! When you know how God treasures you, you will stay away from evil. Anything that grieves God's heart will grieve yours too.

My Bride. No matter how wealthy you are, when a man marries there is a kind of accomplishment that comes with the knowledge that I have committed to this woman, and she is my own. I have paid her bride price just like Jesus died for us. God calls us His bride, and he rejoices over you (Isaiah 62:5).

"And there came unto me one of the seven angels which had the seven vials full of the seven last plagues, and talked with me, saying, come hither, I will shew thee the bride, the Lamb's wife" (Revelation 21:9 KJV).

You are the Lamb's Wife! Praise God hallelujah Amen. As a groom is responsible for his bride, so is the Lamb responsible for you. As a groom is admonished to love his bride, so does the Lamb Love you and died for you (Ephesians 5:25). What else then would He withhold from you? As you live upright and honour His name, He will show Himself strong on your behalf. May we live for Him alone, bringing glory to His mighty name, Amen.

Seclusion

A Secluded Spring; "Secluded (of a place) not seen or visited by many people; sheltered and private." God seeks exclusivity with us.

"And when you pray, do not be like the hypocrites, for they love to pray standing in the synagogues and on the street corners to be seen by others. Truly I tell you, they have received their reward in full" (Mathew 6:5)

The things God seeks us to do with Him alone should be done in seclusion to build intimacy. Prayer is communication between our spirit and His Spirit, just as worship is another realm of intimacy, where all we think of and desire is to please him alone. As a wife yearns to please her husband intimately in marital bliss, so it is with God. That is done in private, in seclusion, from the eyes of the public. No human being in his right mind will make love to his or her husband in the public eye. That is insanity at the highest order. It is a criminal act. Be intentional with your intimacy with God.

> *"And when you fast, don't make it obvious, as the hypocrites do, for they try to look miserable and dishevelled so people will admire them for their fasting. I tell you the truth, that is the only reward they will ever get"*
> *(Mathew 6:16).*

Fasting is another form of building intimacy with God and denying your flesh to nourish your spirit intimately with the one you love. Sometimes we should seek God in prayer, fasting, praise, and worship not to ask for nothing but to just be with Him. Seek His face, as we draw nigh to Him, he will draw nigh to us.

It is said of spring;

> *"Trees and bushes that have lost their leaves over the winter begin to grow new leaves again and also flower in spring. This happens because the temperature of the air and soil starts to warm up and the hours of daylight increase as the days get longer with the coming of spring."*

Are you in your season of Spring? Be Exclusive! It is the beginning of freshness, the newness of life. In your season of spring, when God is doing something new in your life, be sheltered! Learn to be by yourself. Exclusivity, I cannot emphasise it enough.

Anytime God is about to do something new, He calls us alone and out of something(s).

> *"The LORD had said to Abram, "Leave your native country, your relatives, and your father's family, and go to the land that I will show you"*
> *(Genesis 12:1 NLT).*

It is very difficult to discern and hear revelation amidst the noise, around people, and chaos. There are a lot of distractions around us, especially in this age of technology. God is urging us on. If we want to know His secrets be SECLUDED! Until there is a leaving, there can never be a cleaving. May God bless our effort and deliver us from anything that holds us from living exclusively for Him. It is not a boring life to be set apart for God. From experience, it is the most fulfilling human desire one can experience. The knowing that someone has got your back literally, who is ever-present, guiding and leading the way. Who can make everything work out for your good.

A Hidden Fountain

Hidden means "kept out of sight; concealed." This makes me wonder why God is so interested in Singularity? Your individuality makes you different, unique, and original. You are God's masterpiece design for His pleasure and intimacy! You are intricately designed, complicated, and detailed. You are one of a kind. The Collins English dictionary defines a fountain as an ornamental feature in a pool or lake, which consists of a long narrow stream of water that is forced up into the air by a pump. I am reading this, and I am asking the Holy Spirit, how can a hidden thing be an Ornament?

> *"Now we have this treasure in clay jars, so that this extraordinary power may be from God and not from us"*
> *(2 Corinthians 4:7 HCSB).*

You and I are hidden treasures in clay (body). Through Christ refining, we display His excellence, and this is His power at work inside of us. He is the only one who takes the ordinary and makes it extraordinary. He picks the broken and makes it whole. He takes the ashes and beautifies it — all for His pleasure and glory.

> *"A large house contains not only vessels of gold and silver, but also of wood and clay. Some indeed are for honourable use, but others are for common use"*
> *(2 Timothy 2:20).*

May you position yourself in a place where God can use you honourably in Jesus' name. Amen.

A gift can only be a gift when it is accepted and used. We use it to honour and appreciate the giver. Jesus is God's gift to the world. To you and me. How are we using Him? The deep is revealed to give access to the hidden treasures of grace released. Jesus is waiting for us to tap into what He has paid for. Will you arise and take your place among the great? His deep is calling for your deep. Mediocrity is not the kingdom's way of operation!

NOTHING IS IMPOSSIBLE BY THE SPIRIT!!!

GOD BLESS YOU FOR READING THIS BOOK.

I PRAY THE HOLY SPIRIT REVEALS THIS TRUTH INTO YOUR SPIRIT.

I PRAY FOR REVELATION AND A RECEPTIVE SPIRIT FOR YOU IN JESUS NAME.

FOR JESUS CAN ONLY BE REVEALED AND NOT TAUGHT.

MAY HE REVEAL HIMSELF THROUGH THESE WORDS TO YOUR SPIRIT. AMEN.